LIVING

WITH

ADULT ADHD

A Practical, Step-By-Step Guide On How To Overcome Distractions, Lack Of Organisation, And Hyperactivity To Thrive At Work, School, Business And Your Personal Relationships

Sheryl Simpson, Ph.D

INTRODUCTION

If you have just being diagnosed of or have been living with Attention Deficit Hyperactivity Disorder (ADHD), it is quite understandable if you should feel you don't belong here. That is what the world has conditioned you to believe all these years.

Beyond that, it might also look as though your life and career is slipping through your grasp. But it shouldn't be so.

While the world wants you to fit in and be like every other person, it is not in your nature to fit in. And here is why...

What the society has made you to see as weaknesses - the signs and symptoms of ADHD - could be your biggest strengths when properly harnessed.

In the pages of this book, you'll discover why you are different, why your uniqueness is a blessing and not a curse and how you can overcome all the perceived shortcomings attached to ADHD to thrive at your work place, business, relationship and life.

Are you ready to get started? Let's dive in!

CHAPTER ONE

Is This Really ADHD Or Something Else?

Spotting ADHD in children is not always difficult. But that's different with adults. Many adults that struggle with ADHD don't know they have it.

They may not know that many of the challenges they face, including staying organised or being easily distracted stem from ADHD.

Just to help you identify whether it's ADHD or not, here are top 8 signs to look out for:

1.) Trouble Getting Organized:

For people with ADHD, staying orgainsed is a big challenge for them. And it doesn't help in adulthood when one has to juggle many responsibilities; taking care of the kids, providing for the family, meet up with deadlines and on and on.

All these create a complex web for an adult with ADHD making it more difficult for them to stay organised.

2.) Reckless Driving and Traffic Accidents:

ADHD makes it difficult for anyone with it to keep their attention on the task at hand. Spending time behind the wheel of a car is task that requires focus, which makes it a difficult one for them.

Lack of patience and compulsiveness might make the person drive recklessly at a high speed, which exposes them to accidents.

3.) Marital Issues:

Couples can have issues in their marriage. So marital problems are not necessarily a pointer for adult ADHD. But there are some marital issues that are more likely to influence the relationship of those with adult ADHD.

Most times, the partners of those with undiagnosed ADHD may take their poor listening skills, inattention to details or lack of ability to honor commitments as a sign that their partner doesn't care about them.

If you're the one with ADHD in the marriage, you might struggle to understand why your partner is always upset with you, and you may have the feeling you're being nagged at or blamed for something that's never your fault.

4.) Easily Distracted:

In our world today, attention is the new currency. Everything is pulling everyone attention in different directions. To be at peak performance; whether at your place of work or business, requires you shut out the distractions and channel your attention to the important things. And this is where people with ADHD struggles.

If you have adult ADHD, you might realise that phone calls, a beep of incoming text on your phone or email derails your attention, making it especially difficult for you to finish tasks at hand. And this invariably affects your productivity and performance.

5.) Ineffective Listening Skills:

Do you get lost in thought during long business meetings or presentations? Did your partner forget to pick up your child at ballerina practice, even when you had called in earlier to remind him of that?

Issues with attention reflects in poor listening skills in many people with ADHD, which makes them miss out on lots of opportunities, appointments and breeds misunderstandings between them and their partner.

6.) Have difficulties With Relaxation:

Many children with ADHD are usually "hyperactive." Always looking for the next action. They hardly settle.

But in adults, the symptom comes differently. Adults with ADHD, rather than pulling off the roofs, are more likely to be restless; they just find it difficult to relax. This way, those around them always see them as tense or edgy.

7.) Have Issues Starting An Attention-Demanding Task:

It is common place to see kids with ADHD put off doing their home work. But the same can be said of their adult counterpart. Adults with ADHD usually get reluctant when embarking on tasks that require a lot of attention.

Their habit of procrastination always leave them scrambling to meet up with deadlines or hitting their set goal. And this can create problems for them at home, in business or at their workplace.

8.) Emotional Outbursts:

Those with ADHD often find it challenging controlling their emotions. They are usually quick to explode over minor issues. They have this feeling that they have no control over their emotions.

Their angry emotion also tend to go as quickly as it flared, while those who were at the receiving end of their outburst still struggle to get over it.

CHAPTER TWO

Understanding You, Your System And ADHD

Most adults with ADHD know that they are just different from anyone else. Almost everybody - parents, teachers, employers, spouses, and friends - told them that they did not fit in to the popular mold and that they had better change if they wanted to make something meaningful out of their lives..

That said, unfortunately, no one ever told them how to achieve this. In fact, no one ever make them understand that, no matter how much they try, they just can't fit in. And that if they should try to, the only result of that would be failure.

It feels awkward to call adult ADHD a disorder when there are many positive side to it - just that you weren't told or you were told, but not often enough. Those with an ADHD-style nervous system tend to be great at problem-solving. Where you ever told that?

And not just that, they are likable people with a great sense of humor. They are one of the most determined set of people you could ever meet. When they get stuck with a challenge, they tackle it from multiple angles they get the desired outcome.

As a matter of fact, there numerous qualities of creativity, intelligence, problem-solving, diligence and likeability, gives leaves them with a big shot of succeeding at life.

The major challenge for people with ADHD is having to live with the expectations of others to fit in and be like everyone else. Don't let yourself cave into such pressure.

To help you with that, here are a couple of things you'll have to understand about yourself:

Why You Don't Function Well In A Structured World

For the people with ADHD, there is no past, present, and future. Everything is about the present ; the here and now. For this, they hardly think of or learn from past experiences, neither do they look into the future to see the expected consequences of their actions. You most likely act on impulse if you have ADHD.

This is also means that organisation and planning is not your biggest strength. For regular people, every task has a beginning, a middle and an end. But not with you!

Since you can't different between the start and finish of a task, you're most likely to start anywhere and work from there. It's not just in your nature to work within structures, systems and protocols.

Why You Feel Easily Overwhelmed

If you live with ADHD, then you are bound to experience the world more intensely and passionately than the rest of others. Your ADHD nervous system is always overwhelmed by life experiences because it runs on high intensity.

Your ADHD nervous system is hardly at rest. It constantly craves to be engaged in something exciting, interesting and challenging. Your attention is always held in thoughts of what and what and what to do. When you're not hyper-focused - which you rarely are - on the task at hand, then your mind is in different places, seeking for new adventures. Everything is a distraction to you as you attention just easily wanders off it.

Sometimes, you can come out with high-quality work, within the shortest possible time because of your the level of intensity with which you work with when you prime yourself to be ultra focused on task at hand.

You can handle high-intensity situations with aplomb, only to fall to pieces when things become routine again. You live off on high-adrenaline.

Jumping from one high-intense situation to another is hardly a sustainable lifestyle. And while it is part of your nature to crave for such extreme conditions, it can also, at some point become overwhelming to you and those that work with you.

Why You Always Struggle To Get Things Done

People with ADHD have hard time focusing on projects they don't find personally challenging or appealing. This doesn't have anything to do with their ability to deliver on the said task. Just that when they don't find it exciting enough they lose interest.

One of the challenges adults with ADHD face is the struggle and frustration they face when they have that feeling that others depends on them. And when they see themselves as undependable, they begin to doubt themselves and their abilities.

Their mood and energy level also swing according to your level of interest in a given task. When they feel bored or trapped in a project, they can become unease, displeased and reactive.

Why Your ADHD Motors Are Always In Overdrive

If you live with ADHD, chances are, by the time you got to adolescence, the world must have done enough to guilt you into pushing inwards your hyperactivity nature. But doesn't mean to say it's not there.

Now, as an adult, you are still driven forward as though there is a massive engine working inside of you. You might have done well to pick up some social skills to cover this up, but you'll rarely get away with it.

To you, the outside world is not as interesting as the one imagined in your thoughts; the one that makes you want to engage.

Why Timely Information Eludes You

For the ADHD, their mind is like broad and unorganized library. In it is piles of information. This information is there in different forms, picked from diverse sources; articles, videos, audio clips, and what not. They are unarranged and messy.

Little wonder it's almost next to impossible for the person with ADHD to access the right piece of information at the exact time it is needed — there is just no reliable path for locating it.

A working memory should not only have available to it, but should be able to pull up such information when needed. And that's what people with ADHD have to contend with. The information is there, but to gain quick access to it as at when needed is a challenge because nothing is organised in their memory.

Why You Don’t See Yourself Clearly

People with ADHD have little to almost zero self-awareness. While they are good are reading others, it is always a challenge for them to know how they feel in a given moment and the impact of their actions on others.

If someone cannot read what is happening in the moment and does not know has gone wrong or in what particular way it went wrong, the person wouldn't know how to fix it. The same way, if someone with ADHD can’t tell what they’re doing right, they cannot do more of it.

This is not them being deliberately uncaring, inattentive or callous, it's just how they are wired. Knowing this, they should pay extra care to how they internalize the negative feedback of those who don't understand how they are wired.

Why You Have An Issue With Keep To Time

Remember earlier when I told you people with ADHD want everything happening here and now? That's because they don't have a dependable sense of time. For them, there is no concept of time.

And this stems from their quest to always be on the move, with no regard to planning ahead or looking back to reflect on things.

If you have ADHD, time is a useless abstraction to you. It is important to others, but not to you.

Anyway, again, it's how you are wired. And in the preceding chapters you'll discover how you can you can have every aspect of your living in tune and efficient, while embracing the positive qualities of having ADHD.

CHAPTER THREE

How To Always Stay Organized Even With ADHD

As earlier stated, one of the key traits of adults with ADHD are inattention and easy distraction. This makes staying organized a big challenge. If you have ADHD, the thought of getting organized, whether it be at your place of work or home, is very likely to leave you feeling overwhelmed.

That said, you can start with learning to break tasks down into smaller chunks and follow a planned approach to organization.

By following up on your plans and routines, and taking making use of tools such as daily planners, journals and reminders, you can gradually pick up on how to maintain organization and de-clutter your activities.

Here are six tips you could apply now to help make this a less tedious act for you:

1.) Put Up Structures In Place:

To organize your room, home, or office space, start by categorizing your items. Decide on the ones that are important and useful to you, and the ones you'll have to stored away or out-rightly discard.

To help yourself stay organised, develop the habit of keeping notes and to-do lists. Then enforce and maintain your newly organized structure with daily routines.

2.) Free Up Space:

Find out the things that are important to you a daily basis, keep them close. But keep away others in storage bins or closets.

Map out specific areas for things like keys, bills, and other objects that can be easily misplaced.

This will help you free up, not just physical space, but mental space for the things that matter more to you.

3.) Keep A Calendar Or Planner Handy:

To help you remember important dates, appointment and deadlines, always keep a calendar or day planner close.

You can use electronic calendars, to set up timely reminders so you don't miss scheduled events or appointments.

4.) Make To-Do Lists:

A to-do list would help you keep in track of your activities for the day, week or month, so you could easily gauge your progress on how you're getting on with them.

Also use lists and notes to keep track of regularly scheduled tasks, projects, deadlines, and appointments. If you should use a planner, ensure keep all lists and notes inside it. There are also to-do apps you could download on your phone and use to this effect.

5.) Do What You Can On The Spot:

To help ensure you don't forget important things that need to be done, ensure to act on the activities on your list as at the marked time. Don't put things off for later time, that will only leave you overwhelmed in the future once those things are piled up and you start scrambling for time.

6.) Minimise The Paperwork:

If you have ADHD, paperwork is likely to make up a big part of your disorganization. That said, you can put a stop to the endless piles of mail and papers stranding across your kitchen, desk, or office space. To help you achieve that, do these things:

- Put aside time to deal with the mail on a daily basis. Have designated spot where you can easily sort them as they come in. File the ones important. Act on the ones you need to in the moment. And do away with the ones that the content is no longer useful.
- Ask for electronic statements of your transactions and bills instead of physical copies.

- Use different file folders for different types of documents. Label each according to the information it contains so you wouldn't have to go through the heap when searching for any of them.

CHAPTER FOUR

How To Manage Your Time And Stay On Schedule Even With ADHD

Having trouble with time management is a well too known effect of ADHD. It's likely you might have missed count of the times you lost track of time, missed deadlines, procrastinated, or took for granted how much time it would take you to complete a task.

Lots of adults with ADHD expend so much time on one task that they get nothing else completed. And these difficulties can leave you feeling frustrated and inadequate, while making others impatient of your excesses.

But, fret not, there are effective ways you can get hold of your time and manage it better.

Six effective ways you could better manage your time as an adult with ADHD

1.) Have A Clock At Eye View:

You might not like this idea, but get a wristwatch or a wall or desk clock to help you always keep track of time.

When you start a new task, take note of the time. This will help you become more time conscious when engaged with the given task.

2.) Set Timers:

Set limited time for every new task you're to undertake and set a timer to notify you when your time is up.

For more laborious tasks, try setting an alarm to go off at short intervals so as to help keep you informed of how much time is going by.

3.) Give Yourself More Time Than You Would Assume:

People with ADHD are well known to bad at estimating how long it will take them to complete an activity. For every twenty minutes of time you might assume it would take you to complete a given task, give yourself some by adding an extra ten to fifteen minutes.

4.) Plan Ahead Of Time For Appointments And Events:

When writing down appointments to catch and the time of the appointment, do well to give ten to fifteen minutes earlier than they really are.

Then set up reminders to make sure you leave on time and plan to have everything you will need for the appointment handy ahead of time so don't run the risk of forgetting important things.

5.) Prioritise Always:

For those with ADHD impulse control is always a challenge. They have a habit of jumping from one task to another. Completing tasks at hand is a big issue for them. To help you overcome this:

- Decide early enough on what task to tackle first. Start with the most important. And then arrange others behind it according to their priority level.
- Break down large projects into smaller chunks so you don't get overwhelmed in the process.
- Avoid getting distracted by other tasks that would draw on your attention. Stick to your schedule. Work within your allotted time. And resolve never to leave a task until completed.

6.) Learn To Say No:

Don't be quick to accept tasks or projects. A jam-packed schedule can only leave you overwhelmed and stressed out - both physically and mentally.

Do well to check your schedule before accepting any proposal for a task or social event. This will help keep your productivity level high and the quality of your work top-notch.

CHAPTER FIVE

How To Manage Your Money So As To Stay On Top Of Your Finances

Money management takes some budgeting, planning, and organization, and so for people with ADHD, it can be a very big challenge.

Popular systems of money management don't always work for adults with ADHD because they take too much time, paper work, and attention to detail.

For them to manage their money effectively, they will have to create a simple system for themselves which can help them stay on top of their finances. Having such system would also ensure they curb their habit of overspending, long overdue bills, and monetary penalties they pay for missed deadlines.

To help you manage your money effectively, here are the four things you should start doing now:

1.) Control Your Budget:

To regain control of your finances and budgets, you must first make an assessment of your financial situation.

To do this, start with keeping track of all your expenses, no matter how small or big, for a month. This will show you clearly where bulk of your money is going to. And don't be surprised to find out how much you're spending on unnecessary things - especially those impulse buys.

Once you have a clear assessment of your finances and what exactly takes your money on a monthly basis, you can now create out of it a monthly budget based on your income and necessities.

Now that you have your budget, also figure out what and what you'll need to do so as not to go beyond it. This might mean you cooking your own meal often, rather than eating at a restaurant.

2.) Set Up A Bill Paying System:

Try to establish an easy, organized system that will help keep records of documents and receipts that will help you keep track of your bills.

Finding a means to organise money online would mean less paper work and no misplaced receipts for you.

Registering on an online banking platform can help you with keeping record of transactions. You'll get to have handy your list of all deposits and withdrawals, tracking your balance on the go, every day.

3.) Set Up Bill Payment Reminders:

To be sure you don't miss out on due bills, you can set up electronic reminders that will always bring to attention when any bill is due for payment. That way, you can free up mind so you can attend to other important things, while still keeping track of your finances and bills.

4.) Check Impulse Buying:

You don't want to buying everything you see, especially when those things don't fulfill any need and never on your budget list. Doing that places you at the risk of, not just spending beyond your financial budget, but also running into debt.

To help you prevent impulsive buying, do the following things:

- Go shopping with cash only. and leave behind your credit card and checkbook.
- Before going to shop, make a list of the exact things you need and stick to it.
- Keep away from places where you're likely to go on a spending spree, block emails with juicy promotions and offers, and be disciplined enough to stay away from luxury buys you can't afford.

CHAPTER SIX

How To Stay Focused And Productive At Work Even With ADHD

Adults with ADHD face special challenges at their place of work. From organising a project, starting and completing a task and sitting at a place all day long, to listening calmly to directives and following instructions. These things don't come natural to someone with ADHD.

The only way to overcome the challenge of such work place as an ADHD is to your work environment in such a way that it maximises your strength and negates the effect of your ADHD.

To achieve this, here are five thing you should do:

1.) Set Aside Daily Time For Organization:

A cluttered work environment would always leave your mind messy too. To put that right, set aside some minutes in your day to tidy up your office and desk. Having things properly arranged and in their places gives you the mental and physical freedom to jus focus on your work.

2.) Do The Hard Tasks First:

The hard task are the ones that will give you ht highest overwhelm. But instead of putting them off, first take care of them before moving to the lower, less-energy sapping ones. That way you'll stay motivated to finish up as you have already getting the most difficult ones out of place.

3.) Avoid Distractions:

If you can, get a secluded place where you can just be all alone, by yourself, while working on your assigned task.

By all means, avoid distractions. put your phone on silence so you don't get distracted by incoming calls or messages. Also consider getting a noise-canceling head phone to prevent background noise from colleagues and other things.

4.) Keep Journal Of Your Big Ideas:

When you work, make it a point to write down all those ideas that pop off in your head. They don't need your urgent attention and can be a source of distraction to you.

Just to be sure you don't forget any of them, keep a journal beside you where you always record such ideas. That way you can always revisit them in your spare time and rid yourself of the pressure of wanting to jump on them immediately.

5.) Move Around To Keep Your Mind Refreshed:

To prevent you from getting restless during work, allow yourself move around at intervals. That way, you keep your mind refreshed to continue with your work.

While you that, just be sure you're not disturbing others.

If you're in a meeting, try taking down notes and key points. This will help make the whole experience not monotonous and boring to you.

CHAPTER SEVEN

How To Manage Stress And Boost Your Mood As An Adult With ADHD

For people with ADHD, eating healthily, getting a lot of sleep, drinking sufficient water and working out regularly can help you exhibit calm, minimize mood swings, and overcome any symptoms of anxiety, depression, hyperactivity and inattention.

If you're looking to manage your stress level and always be in great mood, here are four things you should start doing now:

1.) Exercise Regularly:

Exercise is probably the most effective way to reduce hyperactivity and inattention in adults with ADHD.

Working out relives your body of stress, boosts your mood, and calms your mind. It will also help you steam off the excess energy and aggression in your system that can get in the way of your relationships.

When exercising, go with something demanding, but also fun. This way, you can stick with it for long period of time without getting bored.

As you work out, also give a shot at relaxing exercises like yoga and conscious walking. Beyond helping you to relive stress, you can also learn how to control your attention and impulses.

2.) Always Get Enough Sleep:

In adult with ADHD, not getting enough sleep can increase symptoms of ADHD, while also reducing their ability to deal with stress and remain focus during the day.

Avoid taking caffeine late in the night, as this would interfere with your sleep.

You would also do well to create a bedtime routine; that's things you do before going to bed at night.

3.) Eat Healthily:

Poor eating habits can worsen symptoms of ADHD in adults. making simple, but effective changes in your meal would help you see a great reduction in various symptoms of ADHD.

Instead of eating bulky food in one sitting, try eating small chunks of it throughout the day. Also avoid sugar and eating junk food as much as you can. Ensure you cook with healthy protein and try to eat fiber-rich whole grains every day.

4.) Practice daily meditation:

Engaging in daily meditation can help you improve your focus, have better control over your emotions, reduce stress, lower impulsive reactions, and resist distractions more.

As an adult with ADHD, chances are your hyperactivity nature would make you struggle with meditation. To help you overcome this, start slowly; meditating for short periods, and gradually increase your time as you get used to it.

CONCLUSION

Now you have all it takes to thrive in a world that would stop at nothing to make you fit in. Go live your best life!

www.ingramcontent.com/pod-product-compliance
Ingram Content Group UK Ltd.
Pitfield, Milton Keynes, MK11 3LW, UK
UKHW022010190726
13853UKWH00004B/1843

9 798537 535669